THE EASY W

TO LEARN HOW TO PLAY

GUITAR CHORDS

by
Christopher Richard

ABOUT THE AUTHOR

Christopher Richard is a musician/producer/songwriter who has over thirty years experience playing the guitar and performing with several Pittsburgh area rock groups and teaching guitar lessons at his studio in New Brighton, PA.

TABLE OF CONTENTS

ALPHABETICAL LIST OF SONGS
(Chords Used)

INTRODUCTION

Strumming chords is one of the most popular ways to play the guitar, and, although there are hundreds of guitar chords you can learn, the simple truth is that there are a handful of basic ones that are used more than all the others. In fact, thousands of songs can be played using the same two or three chords!   It's the truth!

So, whether you are planning to eventually take more advanced guitar lessons and learn hundreds of chords, or you simply want to learn enough to play a few songs for your own enjoyment, this guide will show you everything you need to get started on your own. It is aimed at beginners of all ages with easy step by step instructions, pictures and illustrations to help you play right away, plus, it includes twenty three classic guitar chord songs to play and enjoy!

So, go ahead and get started. You'll be strumming in no time.

CHOOSING A GUITAR

Acoustic or Electric?

It is usually a good idea to start out with an acoustic guitar, if for no other reason than you will not need to buy an additional amplifier or cable to play it. Besides, the method of playing with strings and frets is basically the same for both and you can always invest in an electric guitar later if you decide to stick with it.

The price of guitars ranges from under $100 to up in the thousands depending on several factors, including the quality of the wood, the workmanship involved and the brand name. The most popular choice of acoustic guitars is the classic steel-string dreadnought. Here are a few good choices for an affordable beginner acoustic guitar that are available from Amazon.com.

Jasmine S35	**Yamaha FD01S**	**Yamaha FS800**
Amazon Price: $84.07	Amazon Price: $149.99	Amazon Price: $199.99
ASIN: B0002F58TG	ASIN: B004BUAQEU	ASIN: B01C931H4S

TUNING THE GUITAR

Tuning the guitar is a tricky thing to do at first, since each string needs to be tuned to a particular music tone which involves very detailed adjustments by turning the tuning pegs very slowly one way or the other. It is usually a good idea to purchase a guitar tuner which will show if the string is tuned too high or too low, until it is correctly tuned.

Each string should be tuned to a particular music tone.

1st String = E note (High - Thinnest)
2nd String = B note
3rd String = G note
4th String = D note
5th String = A note
6th String = E note (Low - Thickest)

Turn the tuning pegs very slowly one way or the other to tune the strings to a higher or lower tone.

Many tuners like this one will clip on to the guitar's head and automatically sense the musical tones when the strings are played open (without any fingers on it.). The tuner will show if the string is tuned too low, too high, or correctly in tune.

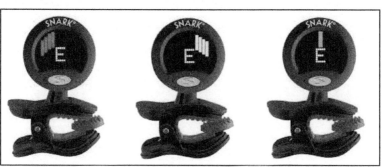

Too Low   Too High   In Tune

GUITAR BASICS
The Fretboard

Most standard guitars have six strings. The 1st string on the guitar is the thinnest one and the 6th string is the thickest.

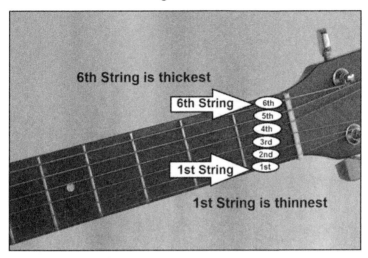

The spaces on the neck of the guitar are called the frets.

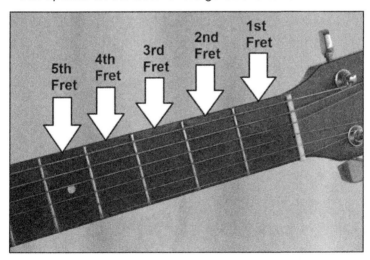

The Strings and Frets on the neck of the guitar are often called the Fretboard.

FINGERS & FRETS

A guitarist's fingers are numbered accordingly, with the index or pointer finger as the first, middle finger as the second, ring finger as the third, and little or pinky finger as the fourth.

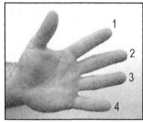
Finger Numbers

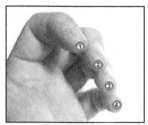
Fingertips

Press and hold your fingertips directly on the strings along the frets, and then pluck or strum the strings with your other hand with your thumb or a guitar pick to make music notes.

FRETBOARD DIAGRAMS

Fretboard Diagrams show a grid which represents the strings and frets on the guitar:

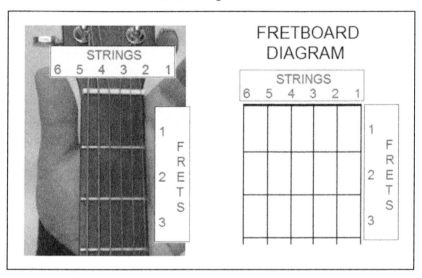

A zero "0" above the grid tells you to play that String "open", or without any fingers on it.

1st String, Open:

4th String, Open:

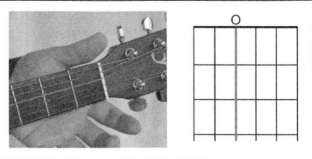

The numbered circles on the grid tell you which Finger to press on the indicated String and Fret.

(**TIP**: Use your finger tip precisely to press down hard on the string and fret indicated. Your fingers may be a bit sore at first, but eventually they will get used to it.)

First Finger on 1st String, 1st Fret:

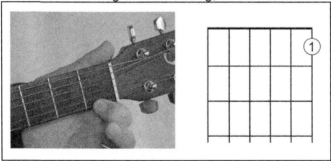

Second Finger on 3rd String, 2nd Fret:

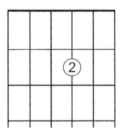

ONE FINGER CHORDS
Mini C & G7 Chords

A **CHORD** in music is the sound of three or more musical notes being played at the same time.

An easy way to get started playing chords on the guitar is to play simpler one finger, or "mini", chords.

Here's how:

Use your 1st Index Finger to press on the 2nd String, 1st Fret,
and then use your other hand to
play or strum the first three strings together at the same time
with your thumb or a pick.

The C chord:

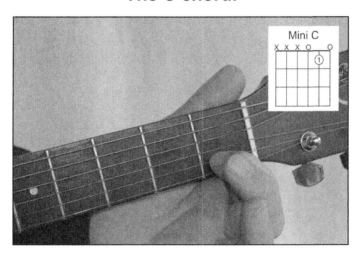

(NOTE: The "O"s on the grid tell you to also strum the 1st and 3rd Strings
"open" together with your fretted finger on the 2nd string,
but the "X"s tell you *NOT* to strum the 4th, 5th or 6th strings
. . . so ONLY strum the first three strings together.)

Later you can try a full three finger C chord,
but for now, this "Mini" C chord will get you started.

The G7 chord:

Play this G7 chord the same as the C chord, strumming only the first three strings together, and NOT the 4th, 5th or 6th Strings.

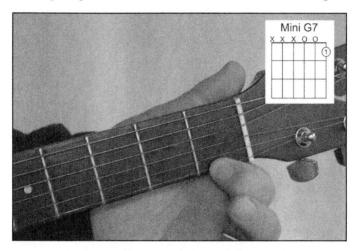

Practice strumming the C & G7 chords several times to get a nice clear sound, changing back and forth from one to the other.

Next, practice strumming each chord four times slowly and steadily, changing back and forth from C to G7.

Strum Marks

Sometimes slashes, or strum marks, are used to show that the same chord should be strummed again, or repeated.

C   C   C   C   G7   G7   G7   G7

. . . is the same as . . .

C   /   /   /   G7   /   /   /

(**TIP**: Keep a slow and steady regular pattern when strumming chords. This is also called keeping a steady **rhythm**)

ONE FINGER CHORD SONGS

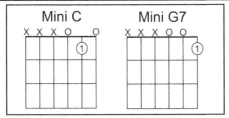

MARY HAD A LITTLE LAMB

C / / / G7 / C /
Mary had a lit-tle lamb, lit-tle lamb, lit-tle lamb,

C / / / G7 / C
Mary had a lit-tle lamb, its fleece was white as snow.

ARE YOU SLEEPING?

C / / / C / / /
Are you sleeping, are you sleeping? Brother John, Brother John?

C / C /
Morning bells are ringing, morning bells are ringing,

C - G7 - C C - G7 - C
Ding ding dong, ding ding dong.

LONDON BRIDGE

C / / / G7 / C /
London Bridge is falling down, falling down, falling down,

C / / / G7 / C
London Bridge is falling down, my fair lady.

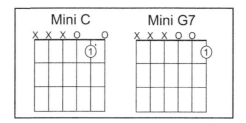

<u>SKIP TO MY LOU</u>

C   /   /   /
Choose your partner, skip to my lou

G7   /   /   /
Choose your partner, skip to my lou

C   /   /   /
Choose your partner, skip to my lou

G7   /   C   /
Skip to my lou, my dar - ling.

C   /   /   /
Can't get a red bird, blue bird'll do,

G7   /   /   /
Can't get a red bird, blue bird'll do,

C   /   /   /
Can't get a red bird, blue bird'll do,

G7   /   C   /
Skip to my lou, my dar - ling.

THE MOCKINGBIRD SONG

```
C              /          G7            /
Hush,   little ba - by,      don't  say a word,
G7             /          C             /
Mama's going to buy you a mock-ing-bird.
C              /          G7            /
And if that mockingbird won't sing,
G7             /          C             /
Mama's going to buy you a diamond ring.
C              /          G7            /
And if that diamond ring turns brass,
G7             /          C             /
Mama's going to buy you a looking glass.
C              /          G7            /
And if that looking glass gets broke,
G7             /          C             /
Mama's going to buy you a billy    goat.
C              /          G7            /
And if that billy    goat won't pull,
G7             /          C             /
Mama's going to buy you a cart and bull.
C              /          G7            /
And if that cart and bull turns over,
G7             /          C             /
Mama's going to buy you a dog named Rover.
C              /          G7            /
And if that dog named Rover won't bark,
G7             /          C             /
Mama's going to buy you a horse and cart.
C              /          G7            /
And if that horse and cart falls down,
G7             /          C             /
You'll still be the sweetest little baby in town.
```

***

THE MULBERRY BUSH

```
C              /              /              /
Here we go round   the   mulberry   bush

G7             /              /              /
The mulberry bush,   the mulberry   bush

C              /              /              /
Here we go round   the   mulberry   bush   so

G7             /              C              /
Ear - ly     in     the     mor - ning.
```

***

ROW, ROW, ROW YOUR BOAT

```
C     /     /     /
Row, row, row your boat

C     /     /     /
Gently down the stream,

C     /     /     /
Merrily merrily, merrily, merrily

G7    /     C
Life is but a dream
```

***

TWO FINGER CHORDS
Em & Asus Chords

Both of these chords use only the 2nd and 3rd Fingers. Place one finger at a time, starting with 2nd Finger, on the proper string and fret, then press both fingers down hard and strum all the strings together.

The Em (E minor) Chord
Put your 2nd Finger on 5th String, 2nd Fret,
. . . then also put your 3rd Finger on 4th String, 2nd Fret,
. . . the 1st, 2nd, 3rd & 6th Strings are also strummed open (O).

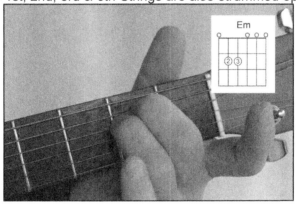

The Asus (A suspended) Chord
Put your 2nd Finger on 4th String, 2nd Fret,
. . . then also put your 3rd Finger on 3rd String, 2nd Fret,
. . . the 1st, 2nd, 5th & 6th Strings are also strummed open (O).

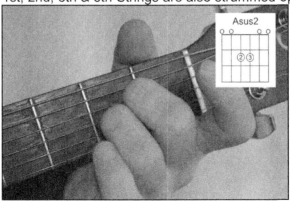

STRUMMING

Practice these strums with the Em and Asus chords:

> Down Strum

Use your thumb or a pick to strum downward across all the strings in a slow and steady rhythm with each count of   "1 ... 2 ... 3 ... 4 ..."

> Down-Up Strum

Use your thumb or a pick to strum down and up across all the strings, keeping a slow and steady "down-up, down-up, down-up, down-up" rhythm to the count of "1 & 2 & 3 & 4 &".

> Strum and Cut

Use your thumb or a pick to strum downward across all the strings, then use the side of your strumming hand to do a gentle but quick "karate chop" to then stop the sound of the strings after you strum them. Repeat with a steady rhythm. (down ... cut ... down ... cut ...)

> Down-Up-Cut

Strum down and up across all the strings and then do a cut. Repeat with a steady rhythm. (down-up-cut ... down-up-cut ...)

> Arpeggios

Use your thumb or a pick to strum down slowly on each string one at a time. You can also reverse and strum up slowly one at a time.

(**TIP**: Repeat each type of strum several times in a steady rhythm to get used to playing songs, changing back and forth between Em & Asus.)

ADVANCED STRUMMING

When it comes to strumming more advanced rhythms on the guitar, two strum patterns stand out because they are so popular and widely used.

> The first is the **Down, Down-Up, Up-Down-Up** strum.

To get started, do the first part of the strum several times:
Down, Down-Up . . . Down, Down-Up . . . Down, Down-Up . . .

Next, strum the second part several times:
Up-Down-Up . . . Up-Down-Up . . . Up-Down-Up . . .

When you're able to do both parts smoothly and steadily,
try strumming both parts together:
Down, Down-Up . . . Up-Down-Up . . .

(**TIP**: Try to keep your arm moving steadily down and up as you strum, especially between the two parts of the strum where your arm should go down without strumming between the two "Ups" to strum up again.)

> The other useful strum is the **Down, Down, Down-Up-Down-Up**.

Once again, the trick is to keep your arm moving steadily down and up to make a smooth rhythm.

Start by strumming steady down strums with a count of
"1 . . . 2 . . . 3 . . . 4 . . ."
Down . . . Down . . . Down . . . Down . . .

Next, keep the same rhythm speed (tempo) but turn your count into
"1 . . . 2 . . . 3 *and* 4 *and* . . .
which becomes Down . . . Down . . . Down-*Up*-Down-*Up* . . .

(**TIP**: These advanced strums will sound great with the Em and Asus chords above and they are used in countless songs, so keep practicing them until they become "automatic" and you can "feel" the rhythm without thinking about the Downs or Ups any more.)

THREE FINGER CHORDS

G, C & D Chords

Place one finger at a time, starting with 1st finger, on the proper string and fret, then press all three fingers down hard and strum all the strings together.

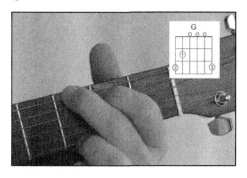

The G Chord

1st Finger on 5th String, 2nd Fret,

2nd Finger on 6th String, 3rd Fret,

3rd Finger on 1st String, 3rd Fret.

2nd, 3rd & 4th Strings are also strummed open (O).

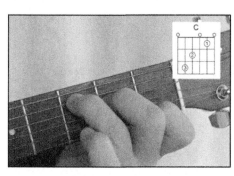

The C Chord

1st Finger on 2nd String, 1st Fret,

2nd Finger on 4th String, 2nd Fret,

3rd Finger on 5th String, 3rd Fret.

1st, 3rd & 6th Strings are also strummed open (O).

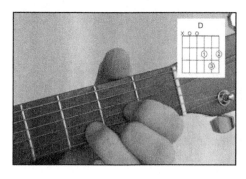

The D Chord

1st Finger on 3rd String, 2nd Fret,

2nd Finger on 1st String, 2nd Fret,

3rd Finger on 2nd String, 3rd Fret.

4th & 5th Strings are also strummed open (O).

Don't strum 6th String (X).

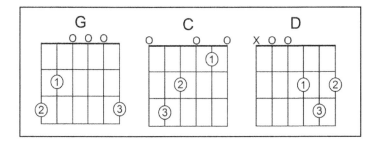

<u>YANKEE DOODLE</u>

```
G              /              /         D
Yan - kee  Do - odle   went   to   town,
G              /         D          /
Rid  -  ing    on     a     po  -  ny
G              /         C          /
Stuck   a    fea - ther   in   his   cap   and
D              /         G          /
called   it   ma   -   ca  -  ro  -  ni.
```

***

<u>AMAZING GRACE</u>

```
    G              /              C              G
A-ma -   zi-ng Grace,   how sweet,   the sound,
    G              /              D              D
that saved,   a wretch,   like me . . . . . . . . . .
    G              /              C              G
I  on- ce,   w-as lost,   but now,   I'-m found,
    G              D              G
was blind,   but now,      I see.
```

OLD MACDONALD

```
G           G          C          G
Old Mac - Donald      had    a    farm,

G          D          G          G
E  -  I  -  E  -  I  -  O.

G           G          C          G
And on this farm   he   had   a   dog,

G          D          G          G
E  -  I  -  E  -  I  -  O.

            G              (HOLD)
With a    bark, bark    here,

            G              (HOLD)
and a    bark, bark    there,

G          G
Here a bark, there a bark,

G          G
everywhere a bark, bark,

G           G          C          G
Old Mac - Donald      had    a    farm,

G          D          G
E  -  I  -  E  -  I  -  O.
```

***

COMING 'ROUND THE MOUNTAIN

G   /   /   /
She'll be coming 'round the mountain when she

G   /   /   /
comes . . . . She'll be

G   /   /   /
coming 'round the mountain when she

D   /   /   /
comes . . . . She'll be

G   /   /   /
coming 'round the mountain, she'll be

C   /   /   /
coming 'round the mountain, she'll be

D   /   /   /
coming 'round the mountain when she

G   /   /
comes.

***

A & E CHORDS

The A Chord

Put your 1st Finger on 4th String, 2nd Fret,

. . . then also put your 2nd Finger on 3rd String, 2nd Fret,

. . . and also put your 1st Finger on 2nd String, 2nd Fret,

. . . the 1st, 5th & 6th Strings are also strummed open (O).

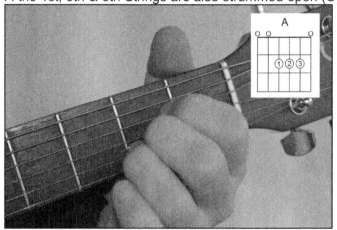

The E Chord

Put your 1st Finger on 3rd String, 1st Fret,

. . . then also put your 2nd Finger on 5th String, 2nd Fret,

. . . and also put your 3rd Finger on 4th String, 2nd Fret,

. . . the 1st, 2nd & 6th Strings are also strummed open (O).

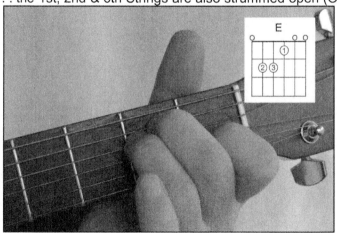

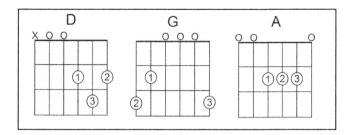

DO YOU KNOW THE MUFFIN MAN?

D   /   /   /
Oh, do you know the muffin man,

G   /   A   /
the muffin man, the muffin man

D   /   /   /
Oh do you know the muffin man,

G   A   D
Who lives on Drury Lane?

***

TWINKLE, TWINKLE, LITTLE STAR

D   A   G   D   G   D   A   D
Twinkle, twinkle, little star,   how I wonder what you are.

A   G   D   A   A   G   D   A
Up above the world so high,   like a dia-mond in the sky,

D   A   G   D   G   D   A   D
Twinkle, twinkle, little star,   how I wonder what you are.

JINGLE BELLS

```
G            /            /            /
Dashing   through the snow . . . . . . .   in a
G            /         C            /
one   horse open   sleigh . . . . . . . . . . .
C            /              D            /
O'er the   fields   we   go . . . . . . . . . . . .
D            /              G            /
laughing   all   the   way . . . . . . . . . . . .
G            /            /            /
Bells   on   bobtail   ring . . . . . . . . . . . .
G            /         C            /
making   spirits   bright . . . . . . . . . . . What
C            /              D            /
fun      it   is      to   ride   and   sing   a
D            /              G            D
Sleighing   song   to - night . . . . . . . Oh,
G            /            /            /
Jin - gle   bells . . . . . . . Jin - gle   bells,
G            /            /            /
Jin - gle   all      the   way . . . . . . . . . .
C            /              G            /
Oh,   what fun      it   is   to   ride   in a
A            /              D            /
one   horse op - en   sleigh . . . . . . . Hey!
G            /            /            /
Jin - gle   bells . . . . . . . Jin - gle   bells,
G            /            /            /
Jin - gle   all      the   way . . . . . . . . . .
C            /              G            /
Oh,   what fun      it   is   to   ride   in a
D            /              G
one horse op - en   sleigh.
```

I'VE BEEN WORKING ON THE RAILROAD

D   /   /   /
I've been working on the rail-road

G   /   D   /
All the live long day . . . .

D   /   /   /
I've been working on the rail-road

E   /   A   /
Just to pass the time away . . . .

A   /   D   /
Can't you hear the whistle blowing

G   /   D   /
Rise up so early in the morn . . . . . .

G   /   D   /
Can't you hear the whistle blowing

A   /   D   /
Dinah, blow your horn . . . .

D   /   G   /
Dinah won't you blow, Dinah won't you blow

A   /   D   /
Dinah, won't you blow your horn . . . .

D   /   G   /
Dinah won't you blow, Dinah won't you blow

A   /   D   /
Dinah, won't you blow your horn.

A7 & D7 CHORDS

The A7 Chord

Put your 2nd Finger on 4th String, 2nd Fret,

. . . then also put your 3rd Finger on 2nd String, 2nd Fret,

. . . the 1st, 3rd, 5th & 6th Strings are also strummed open (O).

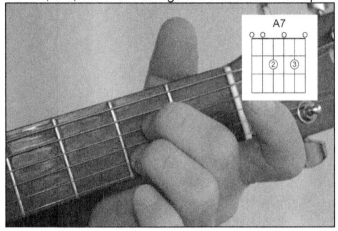

The D7 Chord

Put your 1st Finger on 2nd String, 1st Fret,

. . . then also put your 2nd Finger on 3rd String, 2nd Fret,

. . . and also put your 3rd Finger on 1st String, 2nd Fret,

. . . the 4th & 5th Strings are also strummed open (O),

but do not strum the 6th String (X).

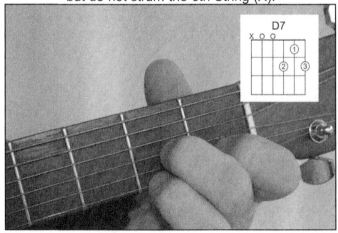

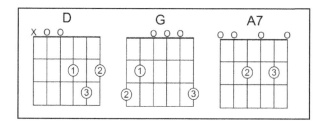

WHEN THE SAINTS GO MARCHING IN

D   /   /   /
Oh, when the saints . . .   go marching

D   /   /   /
in . . .   Oh when the

D   /   /   /
saints   go   march-ing

A7   /   /   /
in . . .   Lord, I

D   /   /   /
want   to be   in that

G   /   /   /
number . . .   When the

D   /   A7   /
saints   go   march-ing

D   /   /
in.

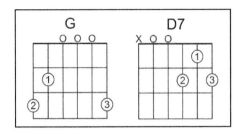

OH, MY DARLING, CLEMENTINE

G / / G / /
In a ca - vern,   In a can - yon,   ex-ca

G / / D7 / /
va - ting for a mine,   Dwelt a

D7 / / G / /
mi - ner forty - ni - ner,   and his

D7 / / G / /
daugh - ter Clemen - tine . . . . Oh my

G / / G / /
dar - ling,   Oh my dar - ling,   Oh my

G / / D7 / /
dar - ling Clemen - tine,   You are

D7 / / G / /
lost and gone for - e - ver, dreadf-ul

D7 / / G
sor- ry   Clemen - tine.

***

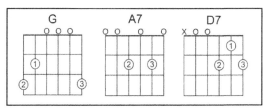

OH! SUSANNA

G   /   /   /
I come from Alabama with my

A7   /   D7   /
banjo on my knee . . .
G   /   /   /
I'm going to Louisiana, my

D7   /   G   /
true love for to see.

G   /   /   /
It rained all night the day I left, the

A7   /   D7   /
weather it was dry . . .

G   /   /   /
The sun so hot I froze to death,

D7   /   G   /
Susanna, don't you cry.

C   /   /   /
Oh! Su - sanna, Oh

G   A7   D7   /
don't you cry for me, for I

G   /   /   /
come from Alabama with my

D7   /   G
banjo on my knee.

C, F & G7 CHORDS

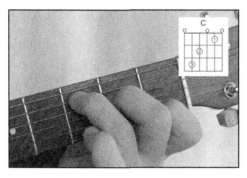

The C Chord

1st Finger on 2nd String, 1st Fret,

2nd Finger on 4th String, 2nd Fret,

3rd Finger on 5th String, 3rd Fret.

1st & 5th Strings are also strummed open (O).

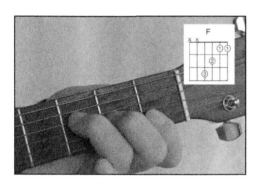

The F Chord

1st Finger on both 1st & 2nd Strings, 2nd Fret,

2nd Finger on 3rd String, 2nd Fret,

3rd Finger on 4th String, 3rd Fret.

Don't strum 4th & 5th Strings (X).

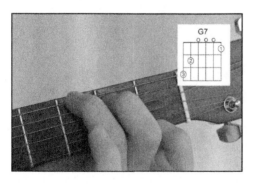

The G7 Chord

1st Finger on 1st String, 1st Fret,

2nd Finger on 5th String, 2nd Fret,

3rd Finger on 6th String, 3rd Fret.

2nd, 3rd & 4th Strings are also strummed open (O).

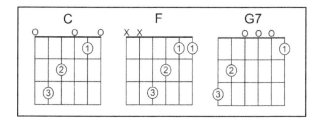

THIS OLD MAN

```
C              /              /              /
This   old   man,        he   played   one,
F              /        G7              /
he played   knick knack   on   my   thumb, with a
C              /              /              /
knick knack, paddy whack, give the dog a bone,
G7              /              /              C
This   old   man   came   rolling   home.
```

***

SILENT NIGHT

```
C              C              C              C
Si - lent   night   . . .   ho - ly   night,
G              G              C              C
all      is   calm   . . .   all   is   bright
F              F              C              C
Round   yon vir - gin,      mo - ther and child
F              F              C              C
Ho - ly      in - fant so   ten - der and mild;
G              G              C              C
Sleep      in hea – ven-ly   pea   -   ce,
C              G              C
Sle - ep in   hea - ven-ly peace.
```

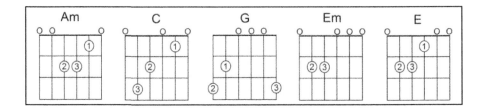

<u>GREENSLEEVES</u>
(What Child Is This?)

```
        Am        C        G        Em
What Child    is   this   who laid      to rest,

        Am        Am        E        E
on    Ma  -  ry's lap    is sleep   -  ing?

        Am        C        G        Em
Whom an -   gels greet    with an - thems sweet,

        Am        E        Am        Am
while shep-herds watch    are   keep  -  ing?

        C         C        G        G
    This,        this    is   Christ  the King,

        Am        Am        E              E
whom shep-herds guard   and an - gels   sing

        C         C        G        G
    Haste,       haste,  to bring  Him laud,

        Am        E        Am        Am
the   babe,   the son    of  Ma   -  ry.
```

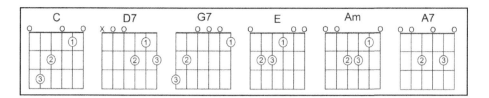

AURA LEE

C   /   D7   /
As the black - bird   in the spring

G7   /   C   /
'neath the wil-low   tree . . . . .

C   /   D7   /
sat and piped   I heard him sing

G7   /   C   /
praising Aura Lee . . . .

C   /   E   /
Aura Lee!   Aura   Lee!

Am   /   E   /
Maid of golden hair . . . . .

C   A7   D7   /
sunshine came along with thee

G7   /   C
and swall-ows in the air.

AMERICA THE BEAUTIFUL

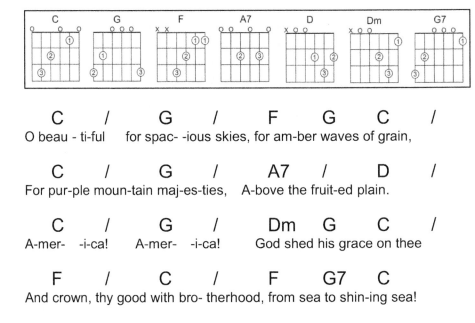

   C   /   G   /   F   G   C   /

O beau - ti-ful   for spac- -ious skies, for am-ber waves of grain,

   C   /   G   /   A7   /   D   /

For pur-ple moun-tain maj-es-ties,   A-bove the fruit-ed plain.

   C   /   G   /   Dm   G   C   /

A-mer- -i-ca!   A-mer- -i-ca!   God shed his grace on thee

   F   /   C   /   F   G7   C

And crown, thy good with bro- therhood, from sea to shin-ing sea!

***

Check out
The Easy Way To Learn How To Play Guitar Tabs!
by Christopher Richard.

CHORD INDEX

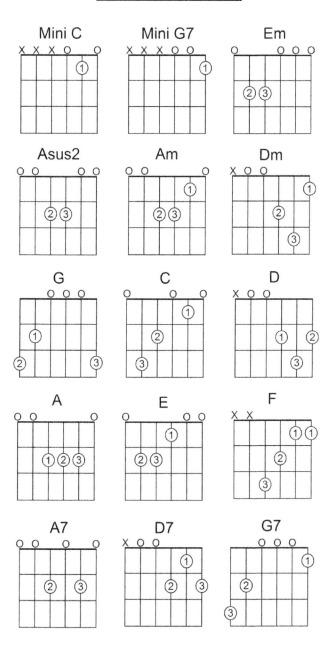

Printed in Great Britain
by Amazon